ROUTEMASTERS IN SCOTLAND
The Late 1980s

David Christie

AMBERLEY

All of the Aldenham repainted vehicles were given this traditional London Transport radiator triangle badge which, as the buses were no longer owned by LT, is surprising. However, as a sign of the refurbishment carried out by LT, it makes more sense.

First published 2018

Amberley Publishing
The Hill, Stroud
Gloucestershire, GL5 4EP

www.amberley-books.com

Copyright © David Christie, 2018

The right of David Christie to be identified as the Author of this work has been asserted in accordance with the Copyrights, Designs and Patents Act 1988.

ISBN 978 1 4456 8676 9 (print)
ISBN 978 1 4456 8677 6 (ebook)

British Library Cataloguing in Publication Data. A catalogue record for this book is available from the British Library.

Origination by Amberley Publishing.
Printed in the UK.

Contents

Introduction

The Author's first sight of ex-London Routemasters in Scotland was in May 1985 when the familiar red London livery beckoned across the fields at Stagecoach's Walnut Grove depot, just outside Perth. Familiar, because I was born in Romford, Essex, just 15 miles from London, where the Routemaster's predecessor, the RT-type, ruled supreme. That is until Sunday workings started to be RM-worked, just before I moved away to live in Central Scotland, in 1973. Upon closer investigation of this 'vision' there appeared to be eight RMs, all still in red livery, most of which were destined to be repainted into the Stagecoach livery, with or without the 'Magicbus' logo. Whether this was planned at the time is open to question as a conversation with an employee proved, when it was mentioned that the eight RMs were to be used on schools and contract work and were to remain in LT livery. Stagecoach was very much a small Perth-based company then and its rise to world domination had yet to begin.

Fast forward one year to May 1986, and another RM vision presented itself one morning on my arrival at work at the Stepps premises of James Buchanan (Black & White Whisky) in east Glasgow. Adjoining my employer's land there was the small depot of Alexander (Midland) which – to a traditional bus enthusiast – had ceased to be of much interest until now, when the familiar shape of RMs parked 'in the fields' again stirred the soul – but this time these RMs were painted into a startling yellow and blue/diagonal stripe livery! A visit and a chat with the manager revealed that they were to be used on Glasgow services and were to be allocated to several garages. The repaint had been done by LT's Aldenham works, resulting in seemingly brand-new buses – although the style and colour certainly were not to my taste!

These Kelvin (as they had now been branded) RMs, after crew training, started to become evident on local services in late June. One had been loaned to Midland proper for use at the Bo'ness Railway opening and another for the Stirling Tourist Service for a short while.

Clydeside was discovered in the Renfrew and Paisley areas in mid-July looking more like London buses with a 'horizontal' livery, without the diagonal stripes and red-based, although the shade was distinctly orangey. Entry to the Dunbar Rally in August seemed to indicate some enthusiasm for the buses as well as explanatory notices inside the RMs informing passengers of their origins. One bus was even turned out in half LT, half Clydeside livery! It was also satisfying to see complete sets of LT-style route blinds in use.

Conversely, the far-flung Strathtay operations in Perth and Dundee were investigated in late August with a visit to Dundee garage which produced the biggest shock yet, livery-wise. Lined up inside the depot were pristine RMs in blue and orange with diagonal white stripes which included white wheels and (almost) a full orange front end. It was that orange front that really jarred and only much later did I discover that the original paint finish was for blue front ends and it was changed immediately before delivery to full orange (bar the top dome) in order to make the RMs stand out from other types in the fleet. It was only in April 1987 that Strathtay redeemed themselves when a new version of their livery appeared with the white stripe and white wheels gone and horizontal bands of blue and orange plus a white cantrail strip making up a far more presentable picture. The RMs were not yet operational at the date of my visit and a further call-in at the Perth depot in mid-October was no different. Finally, on my third try, on 1 November, I found them in service in both cities.

This summary therefore leads me back to Stagecoach and their part in the deregulation free-for-all. Visits to their Walnut Grove depot in late August and late September revealed RMs freshly painted into Stagecoach white with their three bands of brown, red and blue finished off with a chevron style towards the rear of the bus – quite suiting the Routemaster in a modern way, and a far cry from the Strathtay shambles of a livery. It was noticeable that no fleetname was applied – as yet. It wasn't until 31 October that I came across one in central Glasgow running on their 'Magicbus' service complete with that name writ large on their upper deck sides. Stagecoach also operated a few ex-Northern front-entrance Routemasters on their more 'normal' routes and a couple of examples are included in this book.

Come 1993, the Scottish RMs were no more, Clydeside's going first, mostly in September 1990 with company ownership changes, and Strathtay, Kelvin and Magicbus examples all disappearing within the next two years. Actually, many of these vehicles led a charmed life with, out of a total of 234 operational (not counting the fifty or so used for spares), thirty-seven surviving to be exported and a staggering further sixty-two for UK preservation. An example of how a preserved London RM should look is shown in my final section with RM737 attending the Dunbar Rally in 1988 and 1992.

Routemaster Notes

The prototype RM1 was displayed at the Commercial Motor Exhibition at Earls Court, London, in September 1954 but was not tried in service until January 1956. Production started in earnest in 1958/9 with vehicles in service from July 1959. A total of 2,123 'standard' RMs were built up to 1965, with an additional sixty-nine coach RMC versions. Production then changed to the longer RML with eight extra seats, with 524 being built (including a small batch from 1961), as well as an additional forty-three coach versions designated RCL. There were also sixty-five standard-length models built with front entrances for use by British European Airways and fifty-one longer length front-entrance vehicles operated by Northern General – the only instance of Routemasters being purchased new outside of London.

Kelvin

Operating on at least seven routes in the former Alexander (Midland) territory, some eighty-six RMs were operational, with another twelve for spares use. Kelvin's fleet seemed to have lasted longer than others featured in this book, with many withdrawn in 1993. Of the survivors, three ended up being exported, with fourteen going for further use and/or preservation.

WLT 605 (Ex-RM 605) parked up at Stepps depot on 6 May 1986. A touch garish for my traditional taste, the livery was at least well applied, except for the curious continuation to include the guard rails between the wheels – surely these should have been black? No fleetname or vehicle number had been applied – as yet.

RM 605 from the nearside, and in sun, shows the extra nearside rear-view mirrors fitted above the engine compartment. This RM had been outshopped from Aldenham with the earlier style of grille, having the number plate set into a surround. The valances either side of the grille matched, which wasn't always the case.

40 CLT (Ex-RM 1040) passes the bank at Stepps on crew training, 11 June 1986. This RM had the later grille fitted with the number plate set underneath.

RM 229, this time with that fleet number displayed on the bonnet side, also displays the 'Kelvin Scottish' fleetname on the top front dome and just above the downstairs windows. It is here, again on crew training, passing some shops that had seen better days, at Stepps on 19 June 1986.

Midland's only RM! 'Borrowed' from Kelvin to supply a service at the Bo'ness Railway Festival of Transport on 21 June 1986, WLT 538 (Ex-RM 538) leaves the bus station at Boness, looking absolutely pristine with proper Midland fleetname temporarily applied.

A rear view of WLT 538 at Bo'ness, showing the old winding gear in the distance which would, later, be demolished.

My first view of an 'in service' Kelvin RM 22, at the railway bridge at Cardowan Drive, Stepps, on 30 June 1986. This one has blank top front windows, no fleetname on the dome and – a small point – polished sidelight surrounds. The black stains on the radiator are an unfortunate feature which would have been hidden by painting the grille black!

Probably still crew training, RM 371 (note the white fleet number) by the War Memorial in Stepps on 1 July 1986.

RM 371 again, on hire to Alexander (Midland) but this time not displaying the fact, operating the Stirling tourist bus service on 23 July 1986. It is entering Bow Street, almost at the top of the hill to Stirling Castle.

RM 371 leaves Stirling Castle for the descent into the town (as it was then!). This bus survived withdrawal in April 1993 to be converted to open-top by Ensignbus.

RM 471 on Route 301 at Hogganfield on 11 August 1986. Another survivor on withdrawal in January 1993, going to be preserved privately.

RM 770 on Route 301 at Hogganfield looking unmarked, with polished sidelights too.

The rear end of RM 770 at Hogganfield shows a large fleet number applied at the bottom. It will be seen here by the dent on the corner panel that LT Aldenham had not given the buses the ultimate treatment that was the 'norm' for their own LT vehicles – or had been for RT refurbishments back in the '60s.

Finishing up my lunchtime visit to Hogganfield, RM 149 – with fuel filler and radiator stains – was destined, after withdrawal in January 1993, to be exported to Germany.

Here is RM 605 again, the first Kelvin bus photographed (see pages 7/8), which has now been given two 'Kelvin Scottish' fleetnames on the front. It is on route 301 at Ruchazie on 14 August 1986.

This rear view of RM 605 shows another livery variation in the painted-over rear route boxes with a white 'Kelvin' name applied.

An escorted tour of Stepps depot on 20 August 1986 with three RMs in view, the most prominent being RM 229.

Inside Stepps depot, with RM 55 receiving attention (un-numbered with no dome fleetname). An early blank top windows example, it survived withdrawal in February 1993 to be privately preserved. Alongside is LT-liveried RM 716, in use as a spares donor.

A session on Route 5 at Queenslie on 17 September 1986 produced the next four photos with a different look. Firstly, ALM 35B (Ex-RM 2035) is carrying a differently applied livery, with the horizontal yellow band under the downstairs windows much higher. The route blinds are yellow on a blue base and the front dome fleetname is larger. This particular bus was originally built with an offside illuminated advertising panel between decks, which has been painted over here. No 'RM' number is carried.

ALM 72B (Ex-RM 2072) is identical to the previous bus except for the number plate surround.

RM 774 appears to have lost its destination as it stops at Queenslie. Another 'high waistband' variant, it has early blank upper windows.

RM 2035 returns from Easterhouse.

Four images (pages 19 and 20) taken of ALM 73B (Ex-RM 2073) parked at Milngavie depot on 4 October 1986. First off, the varying height waistline yellow strip can be seen in relation to RM 603, parked yonder. Now, this is the first instance with a Kelvin RM to which uneven valances have been fitted – either side of the radiator. The nearside one is of the final pattern, which omits the brake grille indents and curves down to meet the bottom of the grille. The bus looks unused so it must have been part of a recent batch delivered.

The top deck of RM 2073, all looking pretty well refurbished.

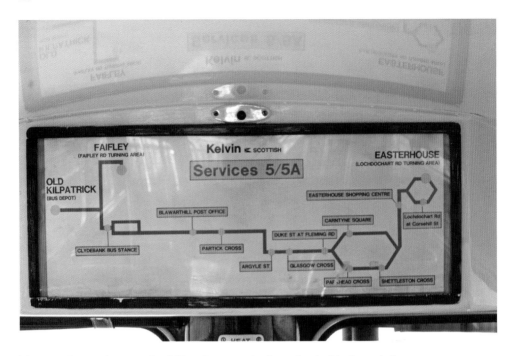

The route diagram for routes 5 and 5A in the case at the forward end of the lower deck.

The lower deck of RM 2073, towards the platform. It seemed strange to a 'Londoner' (almost) not to find the vehicle's fleetnumber by the used ticket box.

Back to route 5/5A with a session for the following six photos on 4 October 1986. ALD 959B (Ex-RM 1959) is seen at Kilpatrick – another offside advertising panel RM. This bus went to (eventual) preservation after withdrawal in August 1987 – an early end to its Kelvin service.

WLT 408 (Ex-RM 408) comes under the Scotstoun railway bridge on route 5A. It was a long stayer with Kelvin, until January 1993, eventually to end up in Sri Lanka!

WLT 471 (Ex-RM 471) shows a nearside view underneath Scotstoun bridge. Seen previously in this book, it was another to eventually go into preservation.

WLT 987 (Ex-RM 987) is 'Kelvin Scottish' free as it passes the Kelvin Hall.

RM 229, followed by another nameless RM (357) on the Kelvin Bridge. There doesn't seem to be much custom for one bus, let alone two! RM 229, seen before, was an export, whereas RM357 was preserved in the UK.

ALM 81B (Ex-RM 2081) at the Trongate, looking pristine – but a pity about that severe dent in the roof! Another offside advertising panel RM with no fleetname, it was bought for preservation when withdrawn in January 1993.

14 October 2016 was the date when I first came across the 'Hop-On' stickers on Kelvin's RMs. WLT 983 (RM 983) is here in Edinburgh Road, North Carntyne, on route 5. This RM went early, in August 1987, to Clydeside for spares.

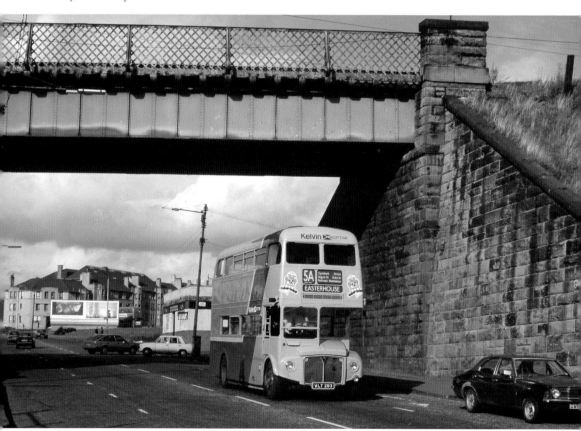

VLT 293 (Ex-RM 293) at Duke Street High Railway Bridge on 16 October 2016 – an early upper front blank window RM. This RM is making do with just one nearside rear view mirror.

ALM 35B (Ex-RM 2035) in Duke Street, Glasgow. This RM was getting to be a 'regular'. 16 October 1986.

WLT 799 (Ex-RM 799) at Gallowgate East on 23 October 2016. It finished up in January 1993, then went to Blue Triangle for further service.

2108 (ex-RM 2108) in a showery spell at Duke Street on 29 October 1986. Paper stickers are being used as the destination box is out of order. Another RM with a single nearside rear view mirror, it was taken out of service early, in August 1987, for transfer to Clydeside for spares.

2072 (Ex-RM 2072) is the next RM to take the turn into Duke Street – it is obviously a problem for sighting as the driver displays.

Numberless WLT 824 (Ex-RM 824) shows odd matched valances (only the second Kelvin RM noted as such) and blank top front windows as it travels along Duke Street. This is the last image taken here on 29 October – and the last on route 5. RM 824 was taken out of service in October 1987 and transferred to Stagecoach Cumberland.

RM 1933 at Garthamlock on route 6 on 5 November 1986. No fleetname on the top dome. This RM was one of the buses repainted into 1933 livery when celebrating LT's 50th anniversary – it appears to have kept its full set of polished lamp surrounds at least! Upon withdrawal in August 1987, this RM returned to London as part of the heritage fleet.

RM 2115 under threatening skies at the corner of Auchinlea Road in Garthamlock. This was the highest numbered RM operated by Kelvin and the third example with one nearside rear view mirror.

RM 2115 passes, giving a rear view showing a nice set of rear blinds for route 6. This RM was transferred to Clydeside for spares upon withdrawal in August 1987.

RM 2072 at Pollok on route 6 on 15 November 1986.

RM 1983, devoid of fleetnames and one of the offside advertising panel batch, in Kingston Street on 9 December 1986. This RM only lasted until August 1987, when it was withdrawn to go to Stagecoach.

WLT 480 (Ex-RM 480) at Milngavie depot on 16 April 1987, looking a bit scruffy. This RM has the full depth valances (matching!) fitted – the only Kelvin bus seen with such.

WLT 678 (Ex-RM 678) at Summerston on route 61. A more usual odd valance situation on this RM.

RM 2086 ends my Kelvin section with a scene in Renfield Street in the city centre taken on 29 April 1987. RM 2086 does not have those 'Hop-On' stickers applied.

Clydeside

Clydeside was formed from part of the Western SMT company and operated at least nine routes, which initially had their own 600 series numbers. These seemed to lose their first digit after a few months. Seventy-eight RMs were operational with thirty-five for use as spares, which seems rather excessive when compared to Kelvin's fleet! Eight of these had been transferred from Kelvin. Most of the RM fleet was withdrawn at a stroke in September 1990 when the company was re-organised. As for the survivors, an incredible twenty-four were exported, with twenty-two going for further use or UK preservation.

My first discovered Clydeside RM, at the Renfrew Ferry terminus of route 605 on 18 July 1986. First impressions of the livery were favourable, with the more traditional treatment compared to the 'jazzy' Kelvin buses. The LT features of black mudguards, black guardrail and brown wheels were retained. Most, unfortunately, seemed to sport a 'Welcome Aboard' slogan writ large on their flanks which spoiled the image somewhat. However, it was good to see the LT 'cantrail' between-decks strip being picked out, although this was wider than LT's, having included the mouldings. The London RM numbers were more strictly applied than Kelvin, and in the proper typeface; this typeface also applied to the route blinds – pure LT! The predominant red (of course) was more 'orangey' than LT's but in some lights wasn't too far adrift. RM 367, upon withdrawal in May 1990, actually went to Kelvin for a further three years before being scrapped. No fleetname had been applied.

RM 73 with no fleetname and no slogan is seen in Renfrew Road, Paisley, again on 18 July 1986, as are the next seven images. The final combination of radiator grille and plain (matching) headlight valances and lower numberplate are contrasted with the blank front upper windows – an early feature. Brightly painted front wheelrings are another embellishment but the nearside trafficator 'ear' is damaged/missing.

VLT 17 (Ex-RM 17) was something of an oddity in the fleet, having many non-standard features. The most unusual were the retention of the original brake grilles either side of the radiator and the full-depth between-decks ventilator, breaking the cantrail. To complete the set, it only needed blank upper front windows but these are the later standard types. Livery-wise, the cantrail is the LT depth, with the mouldings yellow – as also are the mouldings under the top windows. The yellow is also extended to a strip under the driver's windscreen and cabside. There is no fleet number but the Clydeside Scottish name is carried. RM 17 was privately preserved after its September 1990 finish.

RM 37 in Paisley, at the back of the abbey, displaying a different straight version of the Clydeside name.

RM 37 again – an offside view as it passes Paisley Abbey. It can now be seen that the rear wheel centres also received some bright treatment. Shame about the oil stains on the radiator and numberplate though.

RM 465 at Paisley Centre crossroads. No slogan on this one, which was one of the RMs with an odd headlight valance – the later style on the offside.

It seems that the same few RMs kept getting photographed that day – here is the third appearance of RM 37 opposite the abbey in the centre of Paisley.

Another duplicate with RM 73 near the Renfrew Ferry.

The lower deck interior of an unidentified RM at Clydeside's Inchinnan depot. This is the last of my 18 July batch.

RM 441, with blank top front windows and odd valances, photographed in Paisley High Street on a second visit on 16 August 1986. The next four images were taken on the same date. This RM eventually returned to heritage service in London.

RM 444 has the livery differences that RM 17 had, but without the grilles, when seen at Paisley crossroads. This RM was exported to Switzerland.

My old friend RM 73 (last seen on page 36) in the main street, Paisley, had now been given a diagonal Clydeside fleetname and the 'Welcome aboard' slogan, and had had its nearside trafficator 'ear' fixed.

RM 291 at Gilmour Street railway bridge, showing a new slogan on one line – but in large white letters. The offside headlamp valance is mismatched. This RM was preserved on withdrawal.

RM 154 – a blank front top windows example but otherwise of Clydeside 'standard' appearance – at Kilbarchan. This is the last of my images of 600 series routes around Paisley. RM 154 would end up in Italy.

The next five images were taken on 24 August 1986 and are of one bus: RM 416, attending the Dunbar Rally, which was *the* premier Scottish rally event at the time, but is sadly no longer run. It was heartening to see Clydeside's interest in entering one of its newly acquired RMs. RM 416 was chosen – no doubt in view of its lack of dents and, thankfully, with a matching front end! It certainly looks great here as it arrives at the Dunbar site, complete with rear wheel covers (not too apparent in this view). Goodness knows where Clydeside managed to find these – borrowed, I suspect, from a private RM owner.

A peek inside RM 416 to find the London-related notice on the front bulkhead – a nice touch.

RM 416 leaving the rally, seen here a few miles out of Dunbar at West Barns.

RM 416 was duly followed on its return and is seen here under lowering skies at Corstorphine.

The last image from the day as RM 416 leaves Corstorphine. This view really shows those rear wheel covers to good effect. They were a standard LT fitment until November 1971, when an edict went out from LT that they should all be removed – an action that spoilt the RM's (and RT's) looks forever. RM 416 went on to receive a 'half 'London special livery for a year before reverting to normal. After withdrawal in 1990 it went to East Yorkshire for three years but was eventually scrapped.

Two images taken at Glasgow Buchanan bus station on a wet 15 September 1986. RM 154 (seen earlier at Kilbarchan) is about to turn into the bus station on route 36.

Another blank top front window bus, RM 81 displays adverts – a rare thing on Scottish RMs. The polished sidelight surrounds are at odds with the mismatched valances. RM 81, after withdrawal, went for service with East Yorkshire until 1995, and eventually ended up being exported to Madeira.

The next seven images were taken in Glasgow city centre on 30 September 1986. RM 367, the first bus featured on page 32 at Renfrew, is now on route 36, passing the Buchanan bus station. The 'Clydeside' name has been rather inexpertly applied!

Cathedral Street railway bridge, with two very fresh-looking RMs showing the difference between the blank front top windows and the opening ones. RM 641 looks the better of the two without that 'Welcome Aboard' slogan. The larger 'Clydeside' name on both was a much better 'fit' – and a small feature on both was the yellow being applied to the bottom of the cab windscreen. RM 641 ended up being exported to Germany while the RM following, No. 303, just went for scrap on withdrawal.

RM 919 on Cathedral Street bridge, also with large fleetname and the yellow bottom windscreen. The valances however are mismatched.

RM 81 again – the advert bus – in Renfield Street. The mismatched valances really show up here.

Two RMs here in Renfield Street, with reminders of London's famous route 11. RM 245 and RM 1013 appear to be identical except for their destinations. RM 245 went to Kelvin from 1990 to 1993, then was scrapped.

A close-up view of RM 1013, seen in the previous image. This RM was exported to Czechoslovakia.

In the last image from 30 September, RM 874 enters Buchanan bus station. This one has lost its 'Clydeside' name.

The first of two images taken at St Rollox on 3 October 1986. RM 303 (with polished lamps but odd valances) is fairly full as it passes on route 11.

A rear view of RM 245 at a bus stop at St Rollox, with all handrails pristine.

The junction of Argyle Street and Union Street in Glasgow on 4 October 1986, with, surprisingly, the only instance where I was able to photograph a Clydeside and Kelvin RM in the one shot. Clydeside RM 794 crosses with Kelvin RM 2006 at the lights. RM 794 ended up in Canada whereas RM 2006 was transferred to Clydeside in September 1987 for a period before scrapping.

RM 652 near Renfrew Ferry on 4 October 1986 which, if compared to RM 794 in the previous image, throws up quite a few small differences. The legal wording panel shown is block white 'normally', but more recent RMs show just the wording without the panel. The inset step is picked out, as are the wheel centres. The aluminium guard strip on the nearside wheel arch is normally left unpainted but is covered over on RM 794. The big difference however is not the diagonal fleetname or the polished lamp surrounds, it's the RM number in LT gold! This RM eventually returned to London to work heritage services.

Four images taken around the St Rollox area on 10 October 1986. RM 794, at Barnhill station bridge on route 11, displays the same 'Hop On' stickers that had afflicted Kelvin's RMs.

The same RM, but at a different spot at another bridge, with a good view of a youthful conductor standing on the platform.

933 – most unusually minus the 'RM' and also devoid of the large bodyside slogan – exits the same bridge at St Rollox. This RM went for further service with Blue Triangle.

Another slogan-less bus, RM 830 finishes this St Rollox batch.

The following ten photographs were taken on 31 October 1986, from the city centre to Pollokshaws. RM 226 – slogan-less – is in Cathedral Street on route 11. This bus was exported to France upon withdrawal.

The 'odd' RM 17, with the split and narrow cantrail and brake grilles, has now gained original gold lettering for its RM number on the offside – not very visible here. What is very visible is that 'Best Bus' offside slogan in white. The location is Cathedral Street.

Glasgow Bridge, with RM 501 being another RM with narrow (or correct) width cantrail.

Also on the bridge is yet another narrow cantrail RM, No. 219, this one having odd valances and the yellow lower windscreen variation. The Clydeside name is diagonal. RM 219 was transferred to Kelvin for two years before eventually getting back to London as a tourist bus.

Union Street, with RM 303 – the RM with polished lamp surrounds and mismatched valances.

Queens Park – and RM 727 with the other valance mismatched. I can't help feeling that Aldenham could have easily matched up these valances before sale! RM 727 ended up being exported to Canada.

RM 1013 at Queens Park.

RM 951 at Shawlands displays some unusual features, such as the brake grilles that RM 17 had and the large ventilation grille between the top front windows, this time half painted over so as to continue the cantrail without a break. RM 951 also has polished lamp surrounds.

RM 727 at Pollokshaws West station, showing just one abnormality – one odd valance.

The ever-popular RM 17 again, at Pollokshaws on route 10. This is the last of my 31 October batch.

The first of three images taken at Thornliebank on 15 November 1986. RM 794 runs past the school.

RM 104 at the station. A narrow-cantrailed RM with blank top front windows and late pattern valances, this RM went to Southend for two years before being exported to Yugoslavia.

Bright sidelights are the only 'extra' on RM 870 as it completes my Thornliebank sequence.

Paisley's east end with RM 154 (with blank top front windows) on route 36 on 15 November 1986.

RM 694 climbs Johnstone Hill on 15 November 1986. The use of the rear offside stairs space for 'dropping' adverts does nothing for the appearance. This was rife in London at the time but I was surprised to see Clydeside trying it. Not the most attractive of RMs, therefore, in my book.

RM 391 on a wet day at Buchanan bus station, 26 November 1986. The narrow cantrail and blank top front windows and slogan-less sides are notable but it's the extra-large fleetname that catches the eye!

Kingston Street sees my last image for 1986, on 9 December, of RM 367. Someone at the depot didn't have a very straight eye when applying the fleetname.

The first of six images, all taken in the city centre on 11 March 1987. RM 495, arriving at Buchanan bus station, looks neater than with those slogans.

Cathedral Street, with (brake grilles) RM 951. The street is otherwise devoid of traffic, surprisingly.

RM 54 (narrow cantrail) in Cathedral Street, with no 'Hop-On' stickers.

RM 219 in Upper Cathedral Street, with another case of 'stick it anywhere' advertising.

This RM gave me quite a shock as the last time I had seen RM 416 was at the Dunbar Rally – it had now been repainted into half Clydeside and half LT livery! The effect was somewhat spoilt by the over-wide cantrail (including the mouldings) and the adverts.

The rear view of 'half & half' RM 416 shows the darker shade of LT red – and the suitable LT adverts.

Buchanan bus station on 15 May 1987 with RM 206 leaving. This one's got a fancy route diagram plastered on its upper deck. Unusually, the LT triangle badge is missing. RM 206 would be exported to Belgium.

And now for something completely different: an all-over Westcars/Saab livery for our old friend RM 17, seen at Cathedral Street on 17 June 1987.

A couple of shots at Buchanan bus station to end the 'normal' Clydeside RMs. Here is RM 364 on 8 July 1987, now with a side advert fitted and freshly painted wheels. The 'Welcome Aboard' slogan is now looking a bit faded.

Departing on 5 August 1987 is the highest numbered RM that Clydeside operated – No. 2210, which they had just acquired. This has the disfiguring advert space surround that was more or less standard down in London. The 'Clydeside' company name had to find a new area over the first downstairs window – neatly done. No 'Hop-On' stickers either. RM 2210 would end up in Canada.

Two images from the 24 August 1988 Dunbar Rally show three Routemasters: RM 416, now without the half-London livery but given a correct width cantrail; RM 737, restored in LT livery (more of this in the final section); and RML 900, Clydeside's only RML – the 30-foot version of the RM. More of this below.

The three Routemasters lined up, but now the big difference with an RML can be seen – an extra (small) window inserted amidships gives you eight more seats. Finding this bus attending the rally was a big surprise as it wasn't LT's policy (at the time) to sell off this class. Apparently RML 900 was sold with accident damage which Clydeside made good. They seemed to have made an excellent job of it, with different style trafficator 'ears' but retaining the original brake grilles. They even found rear wheel covers for the rally. Pity about the 'Oor Wullie' treatment – somewhat OTT!

These two images were taken of RML 900 (or rather G99 in Clydeside terms) at Largs on 18 June 1992. The bus had lost all its advertising, etc. and was looking very smart. One livery change was with the colour of the wheels, which were now red.

The last Clydeside image – RML 900 would survive to UK preservation.

Strathtay

Strathtay was the smallest of the 'de-regulation' formed companies, with its RMs used on town services in Perth (four routes) and Dundee (two routes). Uniquely, Strathtay formed a separate class numbered from SR 1 for its RMs, which totalled twenty-eight operational and six for spares. Four of these survived to be exported and eleven for further use and/or preservation. A late starter (November 1986), the SR fleet ran until 1990–2, with a few lingering until 1994.

Dundee garage on my first visit, 30 August 1986, with a line of seven RMs closely parked, with more at their backs. The closest two (RM 680 and RM 784) are, of course, still in LT livery and would be used for spares. That leaves ex-RMs 610, 702, 183, 917 and 1017 showing behind, which was quite a sight to behold!

Strathtay's designation SR 16 (Ex-RM 610) is seen in all its 'glory'. The combination of blue and orange is somewhat lurid to start with without those diagonal white stripes and wheels. Then the application of almost full orange for the front (at least the dome had not been included) caps it all. Some ineffectual 'Strathtay Scottish' stickers had been applied, which could have been designed to show white on the dark blue upper deck, and the front cantrail name is barely legible. The only good thing I have to say about this livery is the painting of the guard rails black!

SR 13 (Ex-RM 42), in another part of Dundee garage, shows the small fleet number used, Strathtay choosing not to use the 'usual' bonnet and cabside spots. This example has early blank front top windows with the guard rail 'striped'.

SR13 – and that orange front!

A second try at finding Strathtay RMs in service, on 11 October 1986 at Perth depot. Once again, unused RMs were found stored. Here are SR 19 (Ex-RM 221) with mismatched valances, and SR 18 (Ex-RM 1914) with blank top front windows. SR19 survived to be exported to New Zealand.

A group of five RMs together at Perth garage on 11 October with SR 15 (RM 1874), SR 16 (RM 610), SR 18 (RM 1914), SR 19 (RM 221) and SR 14 (RM 1911). Another eventual export RM here is SR 14, which went to Hungary.

In service at last, at Perth Mill Street on 1 November 1986. SR 11 (RM 743) is on route 2, with SR 10 (RM 427) pulling in. A good comparison between the early and late headlamp valances is shown here. The next nine images were all taken in and around Perth on 1 November 1986.

SR 16 (RM 610) at Perth High Street railway bridge on route 2. Any posters on the front end help to fill in that orange.

The rear view of that livery was always going to be a challenge to the 'designers' – at least it is neatly finished. SR 12 (RM 183) is seen by the High Street goods station.

SR 18 (RM 1914) passes Perth High Street goods station.

SR 13 (RM 42) in Jeanfield Road, Perth. Both this and the previous image show blank top front windows, with SR 13 having the early valances and SR 18 the later type. The application of the diagonal strips seemed to be variable, with the position of the fuel filler in the white band noticeably different on each bus.

SR 13 (RM 42) in the Tulloch Estate, Perth.

SR 11 (RM 743) climbs at the Tulloch Estate.

SR 11 (RM 743) turns at the junction of Scott Street and South Street.

SR 17 (RM 93) about to turn at the junction of Methven Street and High Street. The odd valances are really noticeable here.

SR 13 (RM 42) in Kinnoull Street – the last of the Perth images.

On to Dundee for the last four images of the day with SR 67 (RM 1821) seen in the city centre.

SR 5 (RM 702) near Dundee bus station. This RM survived into preservation.

SR 2 (RM 298) in Dundee city centre. It went on for further service with Blue Triangle.

SR 7 (RM 1691) in a photograph taken somewhere north-east of the city centre. Another RM that was eventually preserved.

The final two images of Strathtay RMs show that redemption is possible! Two newly delivered RMs, on hire to Kelvin and photographed at their Milngavie depot on 16 April 1987, display their more restrained version of the Strathtay livery: gone are the diagonal stripes and white wheels and that orange front. In are straightforward classic lines and the reinstatement of the contrasting cantrail, which sets the rest off perfectly. SR 21 (RM 26) is shown here, this RM going for further service at Reading.

SR 22 (RM 191) is almost identical to SR 21, but for the polished sidelight surrounds. This RM also went to Reading upon withdrawal but ended up back in London on 'Tea Tours'.

Stagecoach
(Including Magicbus)

Perth-based Stagecoach had been running Routemasters (Ex-Northern front-entrance) before this de-regulation occurred but joined the bandwagon with their Glasgow-based 'Magicbus' routes. They ran a total of thirty-four RMs and didn't appear to have bought any 'extra' for spares. A good number of these were saved for preservation, with seven going abroad and twelve staying in the UK. Most of their RMs were gone by 1991.

This was my first discovery of RMs in Scotland, on 25 May 1985, with eight still in LT livery, parked up at Stagecoach's Walnut Grove depot near Perth. Visible here are RM 1596, RM 1611 and RM 1847. All would be painted into Stagecoach's white livery with their 'Magicbus' logo. The rear platform alterations on RM 1611 would be removed. This RM ended up being exported to the USA.

RM 1741 and RM 1599 with others at Walnut Grove. Both would be repainted, with RM 1741 having the Stagecoach logo and RM 1599 as a Magicbus, to eventually be exported to France.

RM 1601 completes this early 1985 batch. It would become another 'Magicbus'.

607 DYE (Ex-RM 1607) fifteen months later, on 30 August 1986 at Walnut Grove in Stagecoach livery, looking quite smart apart from the bashed front dome. This livery, despite the large amount of white, seemed to suit the RMs in a sort of 'modern' way; at least it was a proper design. RM 1607 was eventually preserved.

847 DYE (Ex-RM 1847), again on 30 August, has an identical livery but has the older style headlamp valances. See page 80 for the same bus in LT livery. Both buses went on to run on the Magicbus services.

RM 1571, with an almost undented dome, newly painted wheels, polished lamp surrounds and original fleet number, looks almost smart despite the patched panels and tatty front ads. It is on school contract work, parked at Walnut Grove on 30 August 1986, which was the only time I saw the bus. Whether it got repainted, I know not. I do know that it found its way to Brazil.

RCN 699 was one of at least four operated by Stagecoach of the fifty front-entrance Routemasters supplied originally to Northern General. This one bears the Stagecoach name prominently. It is seen at Walnut Grove on 10 September 1986.

WLT 560 (RM 560) looks a picture, parked at Walnut Grove on 29 September. As previously mentioned, if you are going to have stripes and diagonals, this is the way to do it, in my book. The LT-style blind is interesting, not least as it shows that the RM had been on a local route. The tail end of a red RM is visible yonder. RM 560 would eventually be preserved.

847 DYE (RM 1847) arrives at Walnut Grove on 29 September.

LT-liveried RM 1628 poses at Walnut Grove on 29 September. It does seem odd that no-one thought to cover up those awful remains of front ads.

A visit to Stagecoach's Spittlefield depot on 11 October found RM 1628 again, having come off service judging by its Glasgow route blind – surprising in that state. Unfortunately it is parked right across what must be an ex-London RMA front-entrance Routemaster which I never saw clearly. The Stagecoach-liveried 611 DYE (RM 1611), seen previously in LT livery on page 80, had now had its platform door removed and had a few differences to the standard Stagecoach livery shown so far. The coloured bands at the front had been narrowed to show white at the bottom and had also been 'bled' into the radiator surround, creating a somewhat untidy effect. Improvements, however, could be found in the black mudguards, red wheels and the company name neatly applied.

RCN 695, pictured at Spittalfield on 11 October, was one of Stagecoach's ex-Northern front-entrance Routemasters, but with a difference: this one was purchased ex-preservation, hence the Northern livery. Disastrously, in July 1987 it was destroyed by fire; I well remember finding the remains (there wasn't much left – just enough to see remnants of the livery) at Port Dundas depot, Glasgow, on a lunchtime walk from my nearby workplace.

Two views of RCN 699, another ex-Northern bus, taken on 11 October 1986. This image shows the bus at Perth Mill Street on its service to Stanley. The 'thin-band' livery treatment to the front end has been applied in this instance.

RCN 699 has just arrived at Stanley village.

WLT 504 (RM 504) in Clyde Street, Glasgow, on route 20, 31 October 1986. The 'Magicbus' name now appears large between decks and small on the bonnet front. RM 504 would eventually be exported to Canada.

858 DYE (RM 1858), Stagecoach's highest numbered RM, on Victoria Bridge, Glasgow, on 15 November 1986 on the Magicbus service. This bus has still to have the Magicbus name applied.

WLT 560 (RM 560) at Gorbals railway bridge on service 20. This RM was previously seen freshly painted at Walnut Grove and the new 'Magicbus' name has been added between decks and on the bonnet top. The date is 15 November 1986.

741 DYE (RM 1741) arrives in Cathedral Road, Glasgow, on 11 March 1987 working the 19 express. This RM has the alternative Stagecoach livery seen on RM 1611 on page 86.

628 DYE (RM 1628) leaves Buchanan bus station on 11 March 1987 running on the 19 express Magicbus service. This was the RM pictured still in London livery on page 86.

Port Dundas depot, Glasgow, on 16 April 1987 with a line-up of Routemasters. 628 DYE (RM 1628) is the nearest, with three ex-Northern front-entrance types, RCN 695, RCN 699 and FPT 598C. Stagecoach have replaced most of the original number plates with modern white reflective types.

A pair of Magicbus RMs posing at Port Dundas depot on 8 May 1987. 611 DYE (RM 1611) is in the 'alternative' front end livery and has gained a white registration plate. EDS 50A, mostly in the wider banded front end livery, was registered WLT 560 (RM 560) and has had its radiator assembly changed – the original can be seen on page 90. The one now fitted has a white surround with early type framed registration number and no LT triangle badge. The re-registration to EDS 50A (a 1963 number) seems odd.

Ex-Northern front-entrance RCN 699 in Craighall Road, Port Dundas, on 13 May 1987. This is the same bus that features on page 88, on Perth services. She hadn't weathered badly in the seven months since, apart from the offside scrapes, a rear wheel change (it was red) and the shortening of the company name.

Postscript: London Transport Preserved

The two RMs featured here attended the Dunbar Rally, which was the premier event in Scotland until the mid-1990s, when it unaccountably ceased. I attended the rally on nine occasions and it was only on the last two that I encountered anything LT. RM 737 was at both the 1988 and 1992 events. A 1961-built RM, it had become Harrow Weald garage's 'showbus' in 1980 and passed to their Sports Association from 1983 to 1988, when it was purchased for preservation by the RM 737 Group at Harrow, Middlesex. In 2013 ownership passed to The Red Bus Co., Edinburgh, who have three RMs for special hire. RM 200, the other RM shown, was built in 1960 and was one of the RMs that were sold to Clydeside for spares in May 1987. Presumably nothing drastic was removed as it was purchased for preservation in January 1989 by S. Brydon of Cowdenbeath, Fife.

RM 737 by Drem on the 'Regulation Run' as part of the Dunbar Rally on 28 August 1988. The radiator has been shown as built, with a red central strip and the LT symbol above in place of the triangle badge, which came later. The brake grilles and split cantrail (as a few in the Clydeside fleet) are also original features. It is followed here by Clydeside's RML.

RM 737 at Belhaven, just outside Dunbar. The polished steel light surrounds were a nice touch but not actually authentic, probably having been polished when the bus was a showbus; however, three of the four prototype RMs had them so they were part of the design. Also, the rear wheel disc cover is sometimes embellished by a polished raised circular strip, but not on RM 737.

The rear of RM 737 at Belhaven, with all adverts in the right places. The three polished rear lights show well. Clydeside RM 416 is ahead with another ex-London entrant – a Country-liveried GS.

The date is now 30 August 1992 and RM 737 is again attending the rally – seen here at Aberlady. It looked as though she had undergone a complete repaint with no adverts fitted; there were also no polished lamps this time, making the RM very 'correct'.

Same date, same place but a different RM – No. 200. This RM is a bit of a mixture as the later grille is fitted and the cream cantrail at the front is not split. Lamps are polished, as is the rear wheel cover, but it doesn't have the original offside route number 'window'. All of these things would have been seen in service – but not with the style of fleetname. The block capital 'LONDON TRANSPORT' style did not come in until 1970, when the cantrail colour had been changed to grey since 1965, so a very odd choice for a preserved bus.

RM 200 at Belhaven, clearly showing the block capital LT name.

RM 200 and RM 737 together at the rally field in Dunbar on 30 August 1992. The previously used rally site in the town had now been changed through the building of a new indoor swimming pool. The different front ends of the RMs can now be compared. If only the Scottish companies could have run their RMs in such condition. However, it's fair to say that the influx of so many 'old buses' in 1986 certainly proved an interesting experience for Central Scotland – and especially so for an ex (almost) Londoner like myself!